The Historiography of
ANCIENT GREECE
& ROME

P ATRICK J P HELAN

Tellwell Talent
www.tellwell.ca

ISBN
978-0-2288-8057-8 (Hardcover)
978-0-2288-8056-1 (Paperback)
978-0-2288-8058-5 (eBook)

Preface

History is defined as the study of the past, with the connotation that it is a record of important events, not the trivial. Traditionally, history also has to be written. Any event taking place before the writing of it may be anthropology or archaeology, not history. The concept of oral history would appear to be an oxymoron, but provided an oral statement is contemporary and capable of being transcribed it may be considered reliable history. Anything older than a contemporary statement would run into problems with hearsay.

Historiography is defined as the study of history itself, and how the events mentioned in history have been interpreted over time.

In this monograph, my list of ancient historians is not exhaustive, but represents antiquity as it pertains to Greece and Rome. Not all of the works of these historians has survived, but if historians whose works have survived refer to them, I believe they deserve recognition.

The list of modern historians is much more selective and represents the ones I have found interesting. Again, it was never intended to be complete.

I have included notes on cultural background in recognition of how Greece and Rome have contributed so much to Western culture.

The cinematic notes were my attempt to animate the chronology.

Patrick Phelan
B.A., L.L.B

The Historiography of Ancient Greece & Rome

Cultural background of Ancient Greece

The poetry of Homer whose literary works *The Iliad* and *The Odyssey* reflect Greek myths and legends surrounding the siege of Troy and its aftermath, as well as the fables of Aesop, preceded any works on Greek history by centuries.

Herodotus: The father of History

The epithet was coined by Cicero, the Roman writer and senator. Born in Halicarnassus in 490 B.C., and died 425 B.C. to 420 B.C. He travelled widely throughout the Greek world, including the Aegean and Black Seas, as far back as Egypt. He wrote *The Histories*, much of which concerned the Persian Wars, events which preceded his reaching adulthood and relied strongly on references to the Greek gods and vivid narratives of the glories of Greece. Much of what he wrote was more akin to storytelling than objective and verifiable historical fact. It went beyond "Rumour has it that...", but while the chronology flowed reliably much of his travel stories relied on hearsay.

Thucydides (b. 460 B.C. d. 400 B.C.)

His *History of the Peloponnesian War* does not cover the entire conflict (431 B.C. → 404 B.C.) but ends in 411 B.C. During the war he was an Athenian general sent to Thrace in 424 B.C. The city of Amphopolis was attacked by Sparta later that year. Thucydides sailed from Thasos to raise the siege but upon his arrival the city had already fallen. He was punished for this defeat by banishment from Athens for 20 years. He returned to Athens the year before its defeat, when the city was racked by plague.

It is not known why his *History* ended 7 years before the war did, but we do know his intention in writing it was not simply to record a series of events within a given place and time. Heroes such as Pericles and villains such as Alcibiades are depicted through their speeches, but their strategies come under scrutiny. His work was intended to study the immutable aspects of human nature, to apply to our time as well as his own. It was intended to be, and largely succeeded at being, a study in time which has lessons that are timeless.

Cultural background of Ancient Greece

The playwrights Aeschylus, Sophocles, and Euripides began the history of theatre, more particularly that of tragedy. Aristophanes wrote comedy. These men were contemporaries to Herodotus and Thucydides.

Xenophon (b. 430 B.C. d. 354 B.C)

Another Athenian general like Thucydides but Xenophon was a mercenary with allegiance to Persia or Sparta depending on his employer. He wrote the *Hellenica*, a history of the last years of the Peloponnesian War which starts where Thucydides left off. His *Anabasis*, or the March Up Country, was set in Persia a few years later.

Cultural background of Ancient Greece

The philosophers Socrates, a contemporary of Thucydides and Xenophon, and Plato as well as Aristotle introduced the Western world to the study of philosophy. Hippocrates began the study of medicine. Euclid and Archimedes founded the study of geometry.

Ephorus of Cyme (b. 400 B.C. d. 330 B.C.)

Author of a history of Greece referred to as a series of *Four Sacred Wars* was covering the period of 595 B.C. and ending in 338 B.C., the Battle of Chaeronea. The first three wars concerned the control of Delphi and its temple treasures. These struggles enabled Philip II of Macedon to gain control of Greece. Plutarch says Ephorus received an offer from Alexander the Great to chronicle his Persian campaign, but Ephorus declined.

Theopompus (b. 380 B.C. d. 315 B.C.)

Much of his history of Greece has not survived, save for his history of Philip II.

Ptolemy I Soter (b. 367 B.C. d. 283 B.C)

A childhood friend of Alexander the Great, he became one of his generals in the Persian campaign. He founded the Ptolemaic dynasty following Alexander's death, where he ruled Egypt.

Alexander the Great founded Alexandria, but Ptolemy I built its library. He wrote a history of Alexander's Persian campaign, but it has not survived. Does a historian whose work has not survived remain a historian? I would say yes. This is particularly true since Alexander's Persian campaign is described by the Roman historian Arrian, and many of his sources derive from Ptolemy I.

Timaeus (b. 350 B.C. d. 260 B.C)

Born in Tauromenium, now Taormina, in Sicily. His chronology introduced the system of reckoning by Olympiads, widely used by Greek historians afterwards. Much of his history of Greece and Rome leading to the first Punic War has not survived. But he is from Taormina, which remains a great place to visit.

Cato the Elder (b. 234 B.C. d. 149 B.C.)

The first Roman historian to write in Latin. Latin scholars know him by his saying "Carthago delenda est" which concluded his speeches indicating Carthage must be destroyed. A patrician, he was plain-looking, plainly-dressed, and while he gained a reputation as a soldier, he was known for fighting against Scipio Africanus as much as with him.

His writing began with *"De Agri Cultura"* or *On Agriculture*. He followed with the *"Origines",* a history of Rome.

Polybius (b. 200 B.C. d. 118 B.C.)

Born a Greek, he died a Roman after the Roman conquest of Greece. His *Histories* outlined the Punic Wars with Carthage, a source relied on by Livy.

Quintus Claudius Quadrigarius (b. unknown – d. unknown)

It is believed he lived in the first century B.C. His history of Rome exists in fragments and began in 390 B.C. with the sack of Rome by the Gauls and ended with Sulla c. 85 B.C. He was also used as a source by Livy.

Posidonius (b. 135 B.C. d. 51 B.C.)

Born in Apamea, a Greek city in northern Syria, he was educated in Athens and settled on Rhodes. He also travelled to Spain, Italy, Gaul, and North Africa. He founded a school of Stoic philosophy on Rhodes. A polymath, he studied and wrote on physics, astronomy, geology, botany, hydrology, mathematics, anthropology, history, and military tactics. He studied the calculation of circumference of the earth made by Eratosthenes, and both of their calculations were accurate within 1,000 miles. None of his works are now extant.

His history began where Polybius left off with the fall of Carthage in the Third Punic War. It carried on from 146 B.C. to 88 B.C. We know of much of his works through the writings of Strabo and Seneca. His works were also cited by Timagenes, Diodorus of Sicily, Cicero, Julius Caesar, Livy, and Plutarch.

Diodorus of Sicily (b. 90 B.C. d. 30 B.C.)

A Greek historian born in Agyrium, now Agira, in Sicily. His *Bibliotheca Historica* covered the myths leading to the Trojan War, through to Alexander the Great, and ends circa 60 B.C. It was written in three parts, with fragments and much of the second part covering the Trojan War through to the death of Alexander. His sources included a dozen Greek historians including Ephorus of Cyme, Theopompus, Timaeus, Polybius, and Posidonius.

Julius Caesar (b. 100 B.C. d. 44 B.C.)

As a writer, Caesar's contribution in his memoirs is chiefly military history. His *Gallic Wars* and *The Civil War* were written for political ambitions as much as the historical events they depict, but the direct and clear Latin expression of his work drew praise from his contemporary Cicero, one of his many political opponents.

Aside from his conquest of Gaul, Caesar advanced the territory of the Roman Empire in Egypt, which his successor Octavian would later make official. While fighting in Alexandria, Plutarch reported in his *Parallel Lives* that Caesar ordered fire on enemy ships which spread to shore and destroyed the Great Library.

However, Strabo reported later that the library was largely intact, so Plutarch's claim is now regarded as an exaggeration. Prior to the fire of 48 B.C., political squabbles with Ptolemy VII, circa 150 B.C., caused the expulsion of foreign scholars from Alexandria, and later the Alexandria Library was regarded by Christians as a pagan institution.

Cinematic Note

In the final chapter of Book V of the Gallic Wars, Caesar writes: "There were two splendid fellows in that legion, Titus Pullo and Lucius Vorenus, both of them centurions and both nearly qualified for the first grade."

The names were adapted to the fictional characters in the HBO series "Rome." Although the series contains composite and fictional characters, the main events and major characters are historically accurate.

Sallust (b. 86 B.C. d. 34 B.C.)

He wrote the *Conspiracy of Catiline* which occurred 63 B.C., and the *Jugurthine War* which occurred in Numidia a generation before his birth. A general history of Rome covers, in fragments, the decade to 67 B.C.

Dionysius of Halicarnassus (b. 60 B.C. d. 7 B.C.)

A Greek historian, he moved to Rome and wrote his *Roman Antiquities* in Latin, covering the founding of Rome to the First Punic War. However, the second half of his work beyond 462 B.C. exists now only as fragments. His account of early Roman myths were relied upon by Livy.

Cultural Background of Ancient Rome

Virgil's epic poem, *The Aeneid* follows up on Homer's *Iliad* following the fall of Troy to describe the founding of Rome, written during the time of Augustus.

Roman playwrights did not achieve the renown of the Greeks. The greatest playwright to follow Euripides was probably Shakespeare. Aside from Homer, Greek poets of note are limited to Sappho of Lesbos and Pindar.

Roman poets, however, contributed greatly to Western culture. Horace, a contemporary of Virgil, wrote odes that continue in great regard. Another contemporary was Ovid. He wrote the epic *Metamorphoses* as well as the elegy *Ars Amatoria*. A generation later, the poet Martial wrote 12 books of *Epigrams*, inventing the genre. His contemporary Juvenal wrote the *Satires*.

Strabo (b. 63 B.C. d. 24 A.D.)

Born in Pontus, he travelled widely to Greece, Egypt and other parts of North Africa, and Rome. His *Geographica* was written at the time of Augustus, researched in the Library of Alexandria.

Livy (b. 59 B.C. d. 17 A.D.)

His *History of Early Rome* and *War with Hannibal* were written more in the style of Herodotus. Both histories capture the martial fervour of Rome and are swimming in blood.

Claudius (b. 10 B.C. d. 54 A.D.)

The grandson of Augustus, he was tutored by Livy. Much of his writing was done in the reign of Tiberius, and he became the fourth Emperor. He wrote *Tyrrhenia*, an Etruscan history, as well as an Etruscan dictionary. His *Carchedonica* was a history of Carthage. He wrote a Roman history of the reign of Augustus, and an autobiography. None of his works survive, but are referenced by Tacitus, Suetonius, and Pliny.

Cinematic Note

The British poet Robert Graves translated *The Twelve Caesars* from the Latin of Suetonius to English. He was inspired to write *I, Claudius*, and *Claudius the God*, historical novels published in 1934 and 1935. These were adapted to a popular BBC television series.

Pliny the Elder (b. 23 A.D. d. 79 A.D.)

Another polymath like Posidonius, his first work was an account of the wars in Germania. The work did not survive, but is referred to by Tacitus in the third chapter of his Annals.

He also wrote Natural History, the world's first encyclopedia. This work survived and covers topics such as astronomy, mathematics, geography, anthropology, human physiology, zoology, botany, agriculture, horticulture, pharmacology, mining, mineralogy, art, and sculpture.

You may have noticed the date of his death, A.D. 79, was the year Vesuvius erupted, destroying Pompeii and Herculaneum. This is no coincidence. He was attempting to rescue a friend when overcome by volcanic gases, thereby adding a heroic death to a distinguished scholastic life.

Plutarch (b. 46 A.D. d. 119 A.D.)

Born in Chaeronea, in Greece, he wrote his most important work in Greek, *Parallel Lives*, a series of biographies drawing comparisons of character virtues with flaws of famous Greeks and Romans. This work is very influential to Western literature, but he has been characterized himself as more of a moralist than a historian.

For example, one comparison is the life of Romulus with Theseus, both legendary rather than historic men.

One example of his judgments is found in his comparison of Alcibiades and Coriolanus: "To seek power by servility to the people is a disgrace. But to maintain it by terror, violence, and oppression is not a disgrace only, but an injustice."

Writing in 2022 at the time before publication, can there be a more clear parallel to current American and Russian politics?

Tacitus (b. 56 A.D. d. 120 A.D.)

Perhaps the most famous of Roman historians after Julius Caesar, there is very little known for certain of his own life.

He may have been born in Gaul but was raised a Roman. In 98 A.D. he wrote the *Agricola*, a biography of his father-in-law, the Roman governor of Britannia. He also wrote *Germania*, a description of the Roman frontier on the Rhine. He wrote a Roman history from Galba 69 A.D. to Domitian 96 A.D. The half of the *Annals* that has survived deals with the reign of the three Emperors Tiberius, Claudius, and Nero, 14 A.D. to 68 A.D.

Suetonius (b. 69 A.D. d. 122 A.D.)

A friend of Pliny the Younger, some letters between them have survived. For some years a barrister he became secretary to the Emperor Hadrian for the last few years of his life. He wrote almost a score of works on various topics, but only *The Twelve Caesars* survives intact. Only the three Flavian Caesars, Vespasian, Titus, and Domitian, ruled after his birth, so much of his history would have relied on earlier sources.

Arrian (b. 86 A.D. d. 160 A.D.)

Born a Greek in Nicomedia, he studied philosophy under Epictetus, a stoic. He wrote the *Discourses* based on his studies.

A Roman citizen, he was befriended by the Emperor Hadrian. He was appointed to the Senate, and became a consul. He also led Roman legions in Asia Minor. He retired in Athens and wrote the *Anabasis of Alexander*, an extant work on the history of Alexander's campaigns.

Appian (b. 95 A.D. d. 165 A.D)

Born in Alexandria, another Greek with Roman citizenship, he went to Rome as a young man and became a barrister. His *Historia Romana*, written in Greek, covers the history of various countries incorporated into the Roman Empire with an emphasis on the Civil Wars which led to the end of the Roman republic.

Cultural Background of Ancient Rome

Marcus Aurelius (b. 121 A.D. d. 180 A.D.)

The 20th Emperor of Rome, he wrote *The Meditations*, a work of stoic philosophy. He is known as the last of the Five Good Roman Emperors, a phrase coined by Niccolò Machiavelli.

Lucius Cassius Dio (b. 155 A.D. d. 235 A.D.)

Born in Nicaea, the son of a Roman senator, he wrote his Roman history in Greek. It covers the mythical founding of Rome until A.D. 229. Some of the 80 books of his history are in fragments, but the middle portion is mostly complete, and covers events from Pompey's conquests in the East in 65 B.C. to the death of Claudius in 54 A.D.

Herodian (b. 170 A.D. d. 240 A.D.)

Written in Greek, his *History of the Empire* covers the period from 180 A.D., the death of Marcus Aurelius, to 238 A.D.

Ammianus Marcellinus (b. 330 A.D. d. 400 A.D.)

Likely born a Greek, in the area of the eastern Mediterranean, he served in the Roman army during the reigns of the Emperors Constantius II and Julian. Upon his retirement as a soldier, he moved to Rome where he wrote his Latin history, *Res Gestae.*

His work picks up where Tacitus left off 96 A.D. with the Emperor Nerva. It ends with the death of Valens at the battle of Adrianople 378 A.D. Of the 31 books of the *Res Gestae*, the first 13 are no longer extant. The remaining 18 books cover the 25 years from 353 A.D. to 378 A.D. Even the surviving work suffers from gaps due to corruption and reproduction of the manuscript. His work was used as a source by Edward Gibbon.

177.
THUCYDIDES.
J. E. MAYER OF MUNICH

14

Dumont élève de M.r David.   Lith. de G. Engelmann.

Pline le Naturaliste

Né à Veronne l'an 23 de J. C.
Mort l'an 79 de J. C. en observant l'embrasement du mont Vésuve.

List of illustrations

1. Herodotus	Courtesy of Metropolitan Museum, NY
2. Thucydides	Courtesy of Metropolitan Museum, NY
3. Ptolomy I Soter	Courtesy of Metropolitan Museum, NY
4. Posidonius	Courtesy of Metropolitan Museum, NY
5. Julius Caesar	Courtesy of Metropolitan Museum, NY
6. Claudius	Courtesy of Metropolitan Museum, NY
7. Pliny the Elder	Courtesy of Metropolitan Museum, NY
8. Tacitus	Courtesy of Vienna Courthouse
9. Marcus Aurelius	Courtesy of Metropolitan Museum, NY
10. Townley Venus	Courtesy of British Museum, London

Modern Historians of Antiquity

Edward Gibbon (b. 1737 d. 1794)

His six-volume *Decline and Fall of the Roman Empire* remains influential in Roman history. The work took over ten years to complete. His central thesis for the fall of the Rome was its acceptance of Christianity, which is considered invalid today. He described the Middle Ages as "the triumph of barbarism and religion." His work was admired for its emphasis of the primary sources found in the list of historians previously mentioned here.

Clearly the eastern Roman Empire continued for a millennium after the fall of Rome, despite embracing Christianity. Obviously, a large factor in the fall of Rome was the invasion of the Germanic tribes, along with various internal factors.

Barthold Georg Niebuhr (b. 1776 d. 1831)

Born and raised in Copenhagen, he became a professor of history in Berlin. His *Römische Geschichte* in two volumes was based on his lectures. Prussia offered him the position of Ambassador to Rome, where he studied the works of Cicero and Livy, among others. Years later he completed a third volume of his Roman history which covered events to the end of the first Punic War. His work is credited with the social history study of the patrician and plebian classes.

Theodor Mommsen (b. 1817 d. 1903)

After studying Greek and Latin, he became a professor of Roman law. His *History of Rome* received the Nobel Prize for Literature in 1902. It was published in 3 volumes in the 1850s and covers events leading to Julius Caesar. Other works included Roman law and the study of inscriptions on Roman artifacts.

Lily Ross Taylor (b. 1886 d. 1969)

An American, she became a Latin professor at Bryn Mawr College. During World War II she was an analyst for the Office of Strategic Services (OSS), the precursor to the CIA. Her many works included a study of the voting districts of the Roman republic.

Mariya Sergeyenko (b. 1891 d. 1987)

A Soviet scholar of Latin and Roman social history. She wrote *The Life in Ancient Rome* and also studied and wrote on works of agriculture relying on sources such as Cato the Elder.

Ronald Syme (b. 1903 d. 1989)

Originally from New Zealand, he completed his education at Oxford. He wrote *The Roman Revolution* in 1939, arguing that Octavian saw it necessary to end the Roman republic as imperial Rome was required to restore order. His favourite historian was Tacitus, whose biography he wrote in 1958. In 1964, he wrote a biography of Sallust. A biography of the poet Ovid followed in 1978.

Moses Findley (b. 1912 d. 1986)

An American scholar who lost his post at Rutgers due to the Un-American Activities Committee, he became a professor at Cambridge. He wrote *The Ancient Economy* in 1973 about the ancient economies of both Greece and Rome. His argument that the economy of the ancient world was determined more by social status than market factors has been criticized. Granted that slavery complicated the labour market, but the law of supply and demand remained important factors.

Ramsay MacMullen (b. 1928)

Professor of History at Yale until his retirement in 1993. His works concern social history in ancient Rome as well as studies on paganism and Christianity.

Mary Beard (b. 1955)

A British historian of Ancient Rome lecturing in classics at Cambridge. She has written books on classical art and architecture, on Pompei and the Roman triumph. Her major work is *SPQR: A History of Ancient Rome*, not to be confused with the novel *SPQR*.

She has also done a number of television appearances on the BBC and as such is somewhat of a celebrity, at least in Britain. Unfortunately, her views on modern politics and current events, which she naturally is perfectly entitled to express, have in my opinion distracted from her position as an accomplished historian.

She also has a reputation of a feminist, as most women of distinction today have a wont to do. My wife is a huge fan and insisted Beard be included on this list. I wish to make it clear that she is included as I am also an admirer of her work.

I was particularly impressed with the bibliography in *SPQR*, a portion of a book which my mentors in my undergraduate years always emphasized. Beard writes "The bibliography on the history of Rome is more than any one person could master." I would agree with this as relates to the works of the modern historians listed here, and naturally to the many modern historians not listed here. But as to the ancient historians listed here, from Herodotus through to Marcellinus, I submit that knowledge of their major works is manageable.

Afterword

My father, whose education was inferior to mine, believed that history was merely a collection of stories. My son, whose education in the field of history is superior to mine, believes that history is a study of a particular time and place. With every confidence in my opinion that my father always had in his own, and with due deference to my son's opinion, I disagree.

Teddy Roosevelt once stated in his autobiography that to understand human nature, one ought to read the novels of the great writers. I believe the great historians such as Thucydides, Tacitus, and Plutarch can make a greater contribution to understanding human nature. They portray repetitive themes such that only the names seem to change. Ambition and self-aggrandizement cause many political leaders to be the latest champions of outraged imbecility.

It must have given Strabo some satisfaction to realize that almost every book written in the ancient world existed in the great library at Alexandria. That command of the world's knowledge has been impossible since the Enlightenment. But there is still individual satisfaction to be gained by a review of the ancient classic histories.

Acknowledgements

I owe a debt to some ladies in my life for assisting me with the production of this work. My wife Vivien for her ideas on the cover, as well as her guidance on the list of modern historians. My daughter Kathleen for secretarial assistance, particularly in my struggles with a computer. My long time secretary during the final decades of my law practice, Wendy Gretzinger, who answered the call once again when needed. Nothing gave me more difficulty than the illustrations. My son's common-law wife Lisa Fedorchuk was helpful in that regard.

Manufactured by Amazon.ca
Acheson, AB

13201997R00022